stories
and recipes from

BRYAN'S
BLACK MOUNTAIN
BARBECUE

by BRYAN DOOLEY and LESLIE V. BAY
book design and illustration by LORI COWHERD
photography by DAVID B. MOORE

To Diane
Trust Your Chef!
Bryan Dooley

Publisher:
Bryan Dooley
Bryan's Black Mountain Barbecue, LLC
6130 E. Cave Creek Road
Cave Creek, AZ 85331
www.bryansbbq.com

Printed and distributed by Bryan's Black Mountain Barbecue, LLC

Library of Congress Publication Data
Dooley, Bryan
    Stories and Recipes from Bryan's Black Mountain Barbecue/Bryan Dooley and Leslie V. Bay

For information about permission to reproduce selections from this book,
Contact: Leslie V. Bay via email at l.bay@cox.net

ISBN 978-0-615-55400-6   2011962102

Photography by David B. Moore
Book Design and Illustration by Lori Cowherd

First printing, 2011
Printed in USA

For **Donna, Keely** and **Jack**

Thanks to Mom and Dad for everything, but most importantly for teaching me that anything is possible!

It all began with the great black and white Western movie, sitting man to man with my dad, feet up on the coffee table.

My love of that time period, in the '40s and '50s shaped my life, and here I am, Chef/Owner of Bryan's Black Mountain Barbecue, in Cave Creek, Arizona. Being from Illinois, my life traversed from one side of the map to the other, but I finally landed with my family in a place that I love west of the Mississippi. To be honest with you, if you had said to me that one day I would be sitting here telling you my story of owning my own restaurant, I would have told you that you must have had one too many spicy chile peppers and it has blurred your thinking. After all, I was that shy kid glued to my music, my love of photography and a closet poet.

If I had a movie named after what I am doing, it would probably be *"A River of Sauce Runs Through It"*. Of course Redford would be the director, but my part is not yet fully written, as a restaurant is an ever-evolving process. I like to think of Bryan's Barbecue as one of my children; you nurture them and watch them grow into a fully accomplished adult. The restaurant is one giant recipe with a history, one that tells a story of a chef with a dream, a career path and the choices I have made that have brought me to this point today. I like to say: *"Look back but cook forward"*. Look back to the traditional, but cook with new ways of expressing that history.

History, that's where my childhood mingles with my love of the Southwest, bringing you some of my favorite recipes that I have created over the years. If you think about the life of the chef and the life of the cowboy they are very similar—it's a hard one, with two roundups. For the cowboy it's the annual spring and fall cattle drives. For the chef, it's lunch and dinner, serving a packed house of hungry friends, cueing up for some of the best barbecue that will drive even the tamest wrangler wild.

Grandparents Gene and Evelyn.

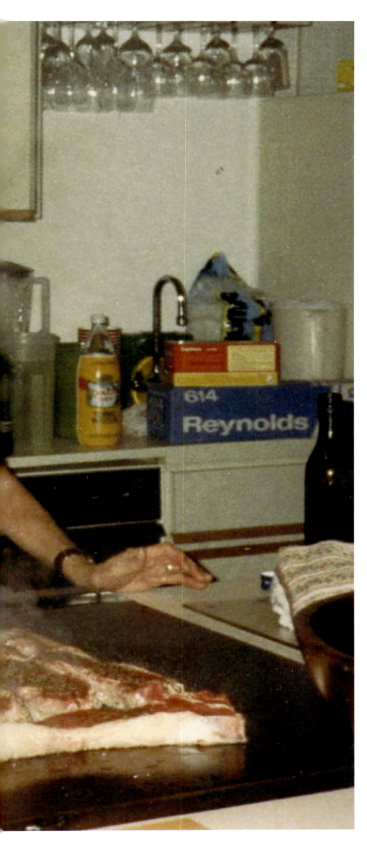

Being a chef is a dream come true for me, it's a proud profession and I like the mystery of the chef's world. It's like being a magician, hold onto your secrets and amaze the world. Heck, what would life be without sharing a few secrets! So I hope you spread the word and share with your friends. That's what made me fall in love with the kitchen, where ideas are endless. Start with a few raw ingredients and the artistic illusion ends up on the plate. Inspired imagination—barbecue style!

I think if you look back at my life, my history will help you understand my enormous passion for cooking. My wife, Donna, and I rode into town with the secret recipe to successful barbecue. Take a heaping helping from my Culinary Institute of America (CIA) training in Hyde Park, NY; add to it 13 years of chef experience at the Fairmont Resort in Scottsdale; mix in my business knowledge and top it off with an enormous serving of down home friendship and you have Bryan's Black Mountain Barbecue.

I am no stranger to the art of good barbecue. Family and food were key and everyone cooked. Both sides of the family brought their talents to the table, but, in particular, I remember my Swedish grandmother, a first generation American who grew up on a farm in Minnesota. She married my southern Alabama born grandfather, bringing them to Chicago, and with them came that southern flair for good barbecue. That's the gene that found its way to me, molding my career.

My grandmother would be in the kitchen creating her signature barbecue sauce with a little bit of this and a little bit of that. Those were great days, and my 'Award Winning' recipes are a result of what she taught me— simple, bold flavors, lightly sauced so the meat stands out. Now that I look back, I was destined to be a chef; I just hadn't recognized it yet, as you will see.

Summers were incredible for me because I wasn't the kind of kid who loved sports, but I did love spending the summers with my grandparents. There was a lake, loads of forest where my imagination could run wild, and a garden filled and overflowing with goodness. When we were all together we would cook. Food was king, and we all loved to pitch into the family gatherings.

My grandfather was a master in the art of barbecue,

so I guess you can say that I had the best pit boss a young cowhand could ever have.

Grampa Gene

First he would have us stack up cement blocks. An old well-worn grill, none of this fancy stuff, would be placed on top of the blocks, creating a smoker that still leaves me able to remember every smell and crackle. I basically learned the concept of what slow, smoked ribs really was and that all came from my grandfather.

When you are a kid you basically think that anything with sauce on it is barbecue. My grandfather taught me differently. He was out there for hours; slow cooking over wood we had collected. That was the real deal and may be the basis of my barbecue style. So you can see, it's all in the genes.

Once we had the pit built, the next step was to collect the hickory from the woods around their house. My job every summer was to follow in their footsteps, collect the wood, hunt, fish and then sit back for some of my fondest memories. The guys would all stand around the fire, *"slap the meat around"* and get all the glory, but it was my grandmother who was an excellent cook. It was her inspiration and cooking talents that helped develop the best barbecue sauce east of the Mississippi. Canning their own barbecue sauce was just one of her many talents. That regard for quality ingredients and the extra time it takes to make something really special is in every dish that I create.

My grandmother taught me so much about the freshness of foods and to enjoy the outdoors while gathering some of the best fruits and vegetables. For my grandmother, it was all about the garden and for me too. I spent time running around in the woods or I would be in the kitchen helping her cook or my grandfather stoke the fire.

Harvesting was the best. We picked every kind of berry imaginable from wild strawberries, blackberries, raspberries, you name it, they all became jams and jellies, and of course, the occasional pie. It didn't stop there. I can still hear that distinctive sound of cracking open her jars of pickles, the crunch, the pickling spices all magic in your mouth.

It was all good stuff; we picked new potatoes that my grandmother would masterfully turn into creamed potatoes with spring onions. If we didn't have it in the garden it was off to the *"You-Pick"* local farms where they had fields and fields of berries and vegetables.

My brother was into sports, which worked well since later in our childhood we moved to a horse farm, a dream for my Mom and Dad that was just outside of Chicago. I was more interested in the artistic stuff. I wanted to draw, listen to music and write my style of poetry. I was that kind of teenager who would lie in bed, guitar in hand playing my music, which was, and still is core to my life today. I must say though, that living on the farm bolstered my love of American history and the old west. Hunting for arrowheads in the surrounding forest kept the dream alive.

As I headed into high school, photography was my plan. I was going to be a photographer and follow in the shadows of Ansel Adams - outside, camera in hand and away from a desk. That's what carried me into college, I was a good photographer and now I had a plan for life, or so I thought.

Photograph by Bryan Dooley

Funny thing is, I went to college never knowing that all this cooking was going to lead me to my own restaurant. As most young bucks, I wasn't sure where I was headed, but I did complete my degree with a bachelor of fine arts from Northern Arizona University, much to the joy of my parents.

So now I was out of college, degree in pocket, but I still hadn't quite found my way. The jobs that were out there were for wedding photographers or possibly architectural photography, but something just didn't click for me. I still wasn't satisfied, so I headed back to the farm for a while to sort things out.

After working my stint at the farm, being a creative kind of guy into music and photography, shoveling *"road apples"* as they are called, pitching in with the hay bales and everything in between for a couple of years, just didn't fulfill my artistic passion and wasn't going to last for long. I've always gone to the beat of a different drummer and this was no exception.

Bryan, at right, and his brother Gene.

If I were going to fabricate a story about how I got to where I am today, here's the way it might have gone. From Chicago I hopped a freight train, being a hobo seemed like the only answer to my destiny. Guitar at my side what else was left? Hopping train to train and crossing the country eating beans out of the can was a far cry from the farm. Migratory work and penniless, walking along the tracks trying to find my way…had you going right? My kind of humor! Well seriously, that might make a better story but here's the truth about my journey to Bryan's Black Mountain Barbecue!

Oddly enough it would take a stranger to suggest the Culinary Institute of America (CIA) in Hyde Park, NY to get my career a jump-start. He was a chef and graduate of the CIA whom I happened to meet along the way because he was the chef for my cousin's wedding. We would strike up a conversation and I would finally tell someone about my love of cooking, and he recognized it too. Who knew, that at this chance meeting he would toss me the challenge of signing up at the CIA to put my culinary skills to the test.

This all brought me to thinking about my life as a kid. I was glued to the Public Television Network, where I watched Julia Child. She taught us all, but at some level, you knew you would never match Julia with a culinary flair all her own. Chef Paul Prudhomme, fell in this category, too. He really heightened my interest in cooking. I was in college when I bought my first cookbook, *Chef Paul Prudhomme's Louisiana Kitchen.* In your heart, you knew that Julia and Paul had paved the road to acceptance into the belly of culinary arts.

So I took the chef's challenge and decided I was going to go to the CIA. Sounds easy enough, all you have to do is apply, right? Well, not so fast, you need restaurant experience and that's one thing I didn't have at all. It never even crossed my mind to work in a restaurant. The time had come and I needed to reveal my gut instincts in the culinary underground. I would hone my skills at a restaurant any way I could, so that I would get into the CIA.

If it was experience they wanted that's just what I would get. I threw my guitar in the back of my car and headed to Texas. Since I had family in Texas and the chef I met was from Texas, it was off to the Longhorn State to test my very inner moxie, my courage, dynamism, well you get the idea. I put my soul to the test to see if this was truly my destiny.

My first job was in Galveston, Texas, at a famous Seafood Restaurant right on the beach. Couldn't get better than that! My love of seafood never leaves me so this was going to be great. The owners and I seemed to connect right from the start—they had a history, a family tradition since 1911 and I liked that, I had a history and a family tradition, too. It was there that I found my passion in so many ways.

I had never been in a restaurant in my life, except as a hearty eater, so this was going to get interesting, but it wasn't going to stop me from being the best I could be. I started out as the grill cook for the restaurant. They threw me right on the line and it was sink or swim. Swimming was my game and I did it really well. I felt good about it. I was a grunt. From there I moved all around, there wasn't a station left untouched, the fryer plus everything in between you can imagine. I was doing so well that soon after that they were having me run the gamut—opening up early, setting up the restaurant, you name it, I did it, and I did it with Dooley flair. I was working breakfast, lunch and dinner, working doubles and triples but,

I fell in love with the culinary scene, and that's not all...

Donna, my wife, was the food checker/cashier. Of course I noticed her right off the bat, but I was trying to concentrate on what was going to become my career.

It turns out that Donna didn't have a car and was riding her bike to work. She began asking me to give her a ride every so often after her shift. Well, we hit it off and spent loads of time together. We had great fun—we were kids living the dream. So for seven months I worked at a restaurant with a gorgeous woman who would become my wife. That's how life's twists and turns never cease to amaze me. Towards the end of my trial with being a line cook, I finally got the letter that would truly change my life. It was from the CIA saying that I was accepted. There was no turning back now. I loaded the car again, grabbed my trusted guitar, and went straight to New York.

I had been at the CIA for a year now and loving every minute of it even though it was filled with stress and hard work. It was my fate, my fortune, my providence —what ever you want to call it the puzzle pieces were all fitting together. I had my first year of school under my belt and it was time for the externship to get my training. By this point Donna had moved to Houston so what better place to train than a fine dining restaurant in the area. This particular restaurateur had several locations and I worked a couple of them. I thrived and did well, stress and all. After six months I headed back to New York and Donna was off to Austin to live with a friend while I finished school.

I did it. CIA culinary degree in hand. It was time to travel back to Austin to pick up Donna. We decided to head to Chicago, back to my parents' farm while I sent out applications to land my first culinary job. My plan was to apply to many different places, our destination of choice - Arizona.

I had to find a job so that I could test out this degree; it's not all lights…camera…action. It's hard work, long hours, and incredibly rewarding when you are doing what you love.

I thrive on the craziness of this business, I chug on through the

middle and don't let it bother me, I have a very even keel—it's an insane business. We were made for each other.

Culinary school may have been the hard part, but getting a job seemed to come easily. I knew I was definitely going to be a chef, so getting a job was the next step. In my own mind I needed to test my skills, my culinary prowess, and above all, show them what I had to offer. I knew that I needed someplace that would really test my soul since I was thriving on the madness of the kitchen. Many applications went out over the great Southwest. From the small resort to the mega resort. Interestingly, many interviews started flowing in, but it was when I talked to the chef at the Fairmont Resort in Scottsdale that it hit me, my juices were flowing, go where there is opportunity and go where I can learn. After all there were banquets, four well-known restaurants and chefs that would bring new morsels of knowledge to me. The revelation came though loud and clear, I could gain so much in one place. There was room to grow.

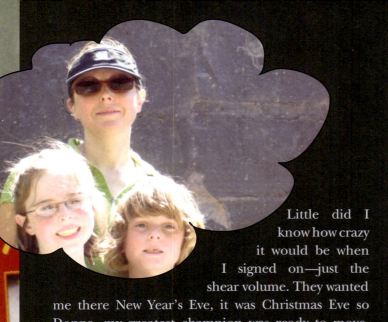

Little did I know how crazy it would be when I signed on—just the shear volume. They wanted me there New Year's Eve, it was Christmas Eve so Donna, my greatest champion was ready to move. And move we did. Once again we loaded the car, guitar in the back seat and off we went, heading to the place I loved the most, Arizona. The great Southwest, home to some of the most incredible landscape and history and only a state since 1912—we were both young but growing.

One thing about me that you will come to know is my loyalty; I was 13 years at the Fairmont Resort Scottsdale. I started as a cook at Marquesa restaurant. I was doing well and after a few months I became an assistant chef for this magnificent Spanish restaurant for three years. Paellas, Paellas, Paellas… you name it; I did it.

After three years it was time to move on, start reaching beyond my grasp, so I took the position of Saucier for banquets. As Saucier, I made the sauces, soups and gravies, for all four restaurants. It made my head spin like a whisk in a bowl. A Saucier has to be able to withstand the greatest of pressures since you are the spine of the restaurants, making the sauces for all the dishes. Above all the sheer volume is staggering when you think of banquets for thousands of guests.

This was a year of complete madness and I thrived. In the resort industry if you are good they keep you moving. Onward and upward I moved to become the Assistant Chef for Las Ventanas Restaurant, which maintained the Southwest Cuisine. I was Sous Chef there for five years. After the five years I was to become the head Chef for a year, it was a great experience, I learned that consistency is so important in a restaurant. Each and every time a guest returns, they should experience the same wonderful meal they remember.

And so the journey of my career continued. From there I headed back to banquets, this time as Chef Garde Manger. That's the hotel business, you just keep moving but the experiences are phenomenal and I was loving every minute of it. My culinary juices were churning. I prized the pressure cooker atmosphere.

Let me tell you a bit about the Chef Garde Manger position. This happens to be one of the most grueling of stations. You have to be on your toes at all times. For four years I was responsible for all the cold foods, cheeses, fruits and every big mirror that ever graced a table at the resort. All the big parties, thousands of people a day.

The best description of Garde Manger Chef is that you are the end result of a plate before the guest sees it on their table. You have to be able to do it all—you mold, you pipe, you spread, slicing and dicing, carving and crimping, tossing and turning, grind and purée - I could do it all day! It's as though your reflection is seen in every mirror on the table, and I was putting in the hours, usually 80 hours per week. But my other love, Donna was not as happy with all the hours. By now we were married and had two wonderful kids.

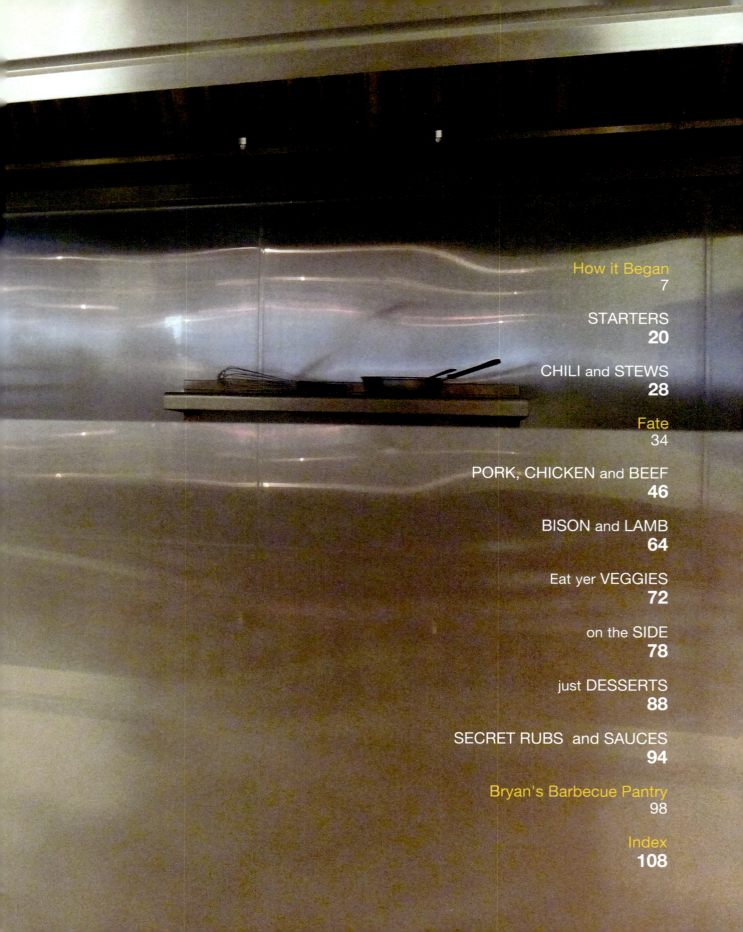

How it Began
7

STARTERS
20

CHILI and STEWS
28

Fate
34

PORK, CHICKEN and BEEF
46

BISON and LAMB
64

Eat yer VEGGIES
72

on the SIDE
78

just DESSERTS
88

SECRET RUBS and SAUCES
94

Bryan's Barbecue Pantry
98

Index
108

THE BIG PIG

(serves 2)

2 large Idaho baking potatoes, French fried
Canola oil for frying
Salt to taste
½ lb warm pulled pork *(page 54)*
½ cup warm Bryan's BBQ Sauce *(page 96)*
½ cup warm Six Pack Cowboy Beans *(page 80)*
2 Sweet Pickled Jalapeños, sliced *(page 78)*
2 scallions, sliced
4 tbsp sour cream
2 fried eggs, optional

STARTERS

Wash and dry potatoes. Cut into 1/4 inch thick strips. Fill deep pot halfway with canola oil. Heat on medium high. When hot, add French fries and cook, stirring to avoid clumping together, about 3 minutes. They should be soft, but not mushy. Remove with a mesh strainer and drain on paper towels.

When done, turn heat on high. When oil reaches 350°, plunge fries in oil and cook until golden brown. Remove from oil and drain on towels. Season with salt to taste.

Place French fries on a plate, and top with pulled pork. Next, top with Bryan's BBQ Sauce, beans, jalapeños, scallions and sour cream. If desired, top with egg, fried to order.

FIREBIRD CHICKEN WINGS

(serves 4–6)
1 dozen drumettes, 2 lbs
1 oz Bryan's Spice Rub *(page 97)*
4 oz Bryan's BBQ Sauce *(page 96)*
4 oz Firebird Glaze
3 scallions, chopped

Season drumettes with Bryan's Spice Rub, place in smoker for approximately 2 hours, or until internal temperature reaches 165°. Combine 4 oz of Bryan's BBQ Sauce and 4 oz of Firebird Glaze in a large sauté pan, let simmer until mixture thickens. Add hot wings from smoker to coat. Top with chopped scallions.

FIREBIRD GLAZE

(makes 3 cups)
8 oz Bryan's BBQ Sauce *(page 96)*
Zest and juice of 1 orange
12 oz honey
6 ea habanero peppers *
1 oz chopped fresh ginger

Combine all ingredients and blend in food processor. Pour into small sauce pan and cook until mixture thickens (careful not to burn) for approximately 5–10 minutes.

* WARNING! *Wear gloves when handling habanero peppers —don't touch anything!*

BEER and PICKLED JALAPEÑO HUSHPUPPIES

DRY INGREDIENTS

1 ½ cups corn meal
1 ½ cups all purpose flour
2 tsp baking soda
2 tsp baking powder
2 tbsp Bryan's Spice Rub *(page 97)*
1 tsp salt
2 tbsp sugar

WET INGREDIENTS

2 eggs beaten
1 cup buttermilk
½ cup beer
3 oz onion finely chopped
2 ea Sweet Pickled Jalapeño finely chopped *(page 78)*

Combine dry ingredients in bowl, then add wet and remaining ingredients.

Form into small balls or use a spoon to drop batter into hot oil, (works well if you dampen hands or use gloves). Serve with our Smoked Tomato Remoulade *(page 77)* and Tabasco sauce.

RIBS of ROMAINE SALAD
with LEMON PEPPER VINAIGRETTE

ROMAINE SALAD

(serves 4)

2 heads Romaine lettuce

Bryan's Spice Rub to taste *(page 97)*

¾ cup Lemon Pepper Vinaigrette

4 lemon wedges

LEMON PEPPER VINAIGRETTE

(makes 3 cups)

1 cup lemon juice

Zest and juice of ½ lemon

1 cup extra virgin olive oil

1 cup canola oil

1 tbsp Kosher salt

½ tbsp ground black pepper

ROMAINE Pick one big bunch of Romaine lettuce, wash and dry the lettuce. Cut in half lengthwise and remove base so that leaves separate. Place on large serving platter and lightly drizzle with Vinaigrette. Season with my Spice Rub and garnish with lemon wedges.

VINAIGRETTE Add all ingredients to a large mixing bowl. Using a whisk, mix until blended. Cover and refrigerate.

BRISKET and BLACK-EYED PEA CHILI

(serves 4 –6)
2 tbsp olive oil
¾ cup red onion, diced
3 garlic cloves, minced
3 tbsp chili powder
1 tsp salt
¼ tsp black pepper
1 can *(28 oz)* **whole tomatoes, crushed**
1 can *(15 oz)* **black-eyed peas,**
   (rinsed and drained)
1 lb brisket, smoked and chopped
   (page 61)
½ jalapeño, chopped *(optional)*

Heat sauté pan on medium high.

Add olive oil, when hot add onion and garlic. Sauté, stirring frequently until onion softens. Add chili powder, salt and pepper. Stir well. Add canned tomatoes with their juice, black-eyed peas and chopped brisket.

Reduce heat to simmer, cover and cook for 30 to 45 minutes to allow flavors to blend. Add chopped jalapeño before serving.

CHILI and STEWS

CABRITO and CHICKEN BRUNSWICK STEW

(Good for a crowd - makes 1 gallon)

1 lb goat meat cooked & pulled
1 lb chicken meat cooked & pulled
3 qts chicken or goat stock
1 ea 28 oz can crushed tomatoes
1 ea red onion chopped
8 oz fingerling potatoes quartered
1 lb lima beans
1 lb corn
1 ea clove garlic chopped
1 ea 12 oz beer
1 tsp Bryan's Spice Rub *(page 97)*
2 tsp cider vinegar
1 tsp Worcestershire sauce
Salt and black pepper
4 oz olive oil
4 oz flour

In large pot sweat onions and garlic in olive oil. Add spice rub and flour. Stir until flour and oil are blended be careful not to burn. Add beer, stock, stir with whisk to remove lumps. Add remaining ingredients except for meat, and stir. Let stew simmer for about 45 minutes. Add meat and adjust seasoning with salt and pepper. Simmer an additional 15 minutes.

One of our typical family gatherings.

Grandma Evelyn, above and at right.

SHRIMP EVELYN

(serves 6-8)

1 tbsp olive oil

4 tbsp butter

1 cup diced red onion

1 cup diced celery

1 cup diced red bell pepper

4 cloves garlic, peeled and chopped

8 tbsp Bryan's Spice Rub *(page 97)*

6 oz beer

2 lbs shrimp, shell on and veins removed *

2 tomatoes, chopped

Juice of 2 lemons

Loaf of crusty bread

Heat large, deep skillet on medium heat. Add olive oil and butter. When hot, add onion, celery and bell pepper. Sauté about 5–7 minutes, or until the vegetables are soft. Add beer, garlic and Bryan's Spice Rub to pan. Simmer until liquid is reduced in half. Add shrimp and cook until shells turn pink, about 3–5 minutes. Top with tomatoes and finish with lemon juice. Serve with crusty loaf.

* To devein, run knife through shell on back, rinse vein - shell remains.

This makes a delightful family style dish served over rice as a main course.

It was fate that brought me to open my restaurant. I truly believe that as fact. I was trying to spend more time with the kids. I decided we were going ice skating in the desert. We all donned our skates, headed for the great indoor rink, where we would wile away the hours in family bliss.

My son challenged me to a race. Simple enough, after all I was the great Chef who could make a flower out of a tiny radish, how hard could this be? Wrong! We flew around the rink, me chasing with the greatest of ease until be both tripped, we tumbled, well actually I did—head over heels we went, spinning and sliding. At first I was sure this was just a bad sprain, I would hobble home, get some rest and voilà all would be fine with the world.

It wasn't until the morning, when I went to get out of bed and met the floor face first, that I realized that the leg was definitely broken. Off to the hospital to have this all checked out. It was worse than I thought. After seeing the doc who wanted to fill my leg with pins and you name it, I decided this must be a bit more than I thought, but I was strong. I would resist the pins and an operation and get a cast, letting it heal on its own - no pins for this chef.

The leg really sidelined me for six months. After a while, the cast began to drive me insane. The claustrophobia of having it on was making me crazy. All night I would pace the halls up and down, thumping the floor with the sound of the cast and crutches. By this point, Donna said, *"This is it. You are through with these long hours. This is your chance. Take it and start your restaurant."* Donna, is the love of my life and the driving force behind Bryan's Black Mountain Barbecue.

Donna had to do something because this broken leg gave us too much time to think! In April of 2009, after years of thought and with my wife Donna at my side, forever collecting ideas and items for a restaurant that was only a dream, now was the time that allowed us to add another American legend to Western history; a chef with a passion for Barbecue and the enduring feel for the preservation of the old west, but with a brand all my own, a new west style barbecue.

I like to think of taking the American old west and turning my culinary talents into the modern cowboy new west style. Being the lover of the west and all its lore, I'd like to say we saddled up and hit the trail, it was kind of like that, only it was Donna who led the gang. Piling me into the car, leg out the window, we rode up and down the main drag of Cave Creek, looking for just the right spot.

Now you have to understand Cave Creek. There basically is only one drag—it's kind of like Marshall Dillon's Dodge City. You have your historic tourist spots, the old west look, the cowboy bars and honky-tonks, even the bull riding on the weekend's…ahhh what's not to love about that.

Everyday we would drive up and down, looking for just the right spot. There it was, behind a row of shops, a tiny historic block house set up on a hill. We started to get the picture of what we could do. We would build a patio going all around the front, put old wood picnic tables out front and a huge smoker inside. This was going to be a family place where everyone would want to hang out—have a beer and bbq like they had never tasted before. In the meantime, while I was laid-up, I was testing all my great ideas on my friends and neighbors. Beans, rubs, potato salad and my famous barbecue sauce *"Bryan-Style"*. None of this sticky sweet sauce for me - so far so good, rave reviews.

On one fateful day we went back to see our little bungalow. As it happened, we found out that the whole center in front of the house was now for sale. My dad was in town at that time, so we drove him by to see what he thought. We walked all around; the possibilities were endless. The end unit, formerly a gallery held my dream of Bryan's Barbecue within its four walls. It didn't take long, my Dad and I formed a partnership and purchased the entire center. No time to look back now, it was time to send up *"Barbecue Smoke Signals"* in the town of Cave Creek. Bryan's Black Mountain Barbecue was coming soon. Two years in the making, we gathered every dream and put together our first restaurant.

After purchasing Las Tiendas in Cave Creek, Donna and I would make a home for Bryan's Black Mountain Barbecue. This was it—we were like the old homesteaders of the Southwest. We had our patch of land and now we had to build our dream from whatever ideas and hard work we could muster up. The freedom to create our new frontier was before us and we started in with all the gusto of the modern American families of the West.

Fitting the *"cowboy west"* into the feel of Cave Creek with a clean modern look—or as we like to call it *"clean cowboy"* was going to be paramount to the development of

Bryan's Black Mountain Barbecue. Much of the atmosphere and style inside is the work we designed ourselves. Years of dreaming—the images, the sites, the sounds and the sensations were now becoming a reality.

We chose the end building to be our location and it needed everything to be changed on the interior, so that the character could grow and be nurtured. There was work to be done and this was now our full time job.

From the time we actually started looking for the right homestead to the opening of the doors, it would be two years in the making. We would juggle family, friends and work, but we would do this—I believed in myself and my recipes and the rest would come.

Building a restaurant is so much more than that picture you have in your mind and so many changes and bumps come along the way. Permits, architects, kitchen design, town permits, town approval and all the quirks and kinks to work out, but you plug along day-by-day, loving every minute of your new life and newfound freedom.

I didn't have a horse but I had my trusted old Jeep to take me to and from the job. Kind of like Roy Rogers and Dale Evans, they had old Nellie Bell, and who could beat Trigger. I add this part in because everyone needs a trusted steed at your side and for me it was my beloved Jeep. To this day, she is still at my side, a little worse for the wear, but humming right along beside me. The old west cowboy and myself had a lot in common - resilience, determination, individualism and very little time to do anything but work to maintain our livelihood.

The actual building that was to become the now famous Bryan's Black Mountain Barbecue needed an entire overhaul on the interior, the exterior looked great since the previous owner had just completed its renovation. We wasted no time and jumped right in. It was a whirlwind of magnificent action. I couldn't wait for the time when I would stoke up the flames of the smoker and the plumes of smoke would fill the town with goodness.

Let me get the door and you can have a look around and see how the frenzy unfolded. Where do you begin is the question— everywhere you looked there were things to be done. The kitchen came first, after all that is the very heart of the business.

First thing to go was a solid wall that divided what would become my constant companion, the one whose job it is to follow the other in their path – the kitchen, front of the house, my stage to the enthusiastic lover of barbecue.

Walls came down and walls went up. We began by cutting through an interior wall so that we would have the service windows that would open up the restaurant itself. The idea of a family friendly warm atmosphere, where you could come up, place an order, talk to the chef, and above all, *"Trust Your Chef"* was

paramount in the design and layout. So the demolition began, knocking out two large cutout window areas so we would be able to interact with our guests. After placing the order, you would be able to walk down past a long open area to the kitchen, where you would pick up your order. Here you would be able to shout out a *"hello"* to me and my gang of hard working wranglers.

The next wall to go in was the wall that needed to be installed to separate the kitchen from what would become an additional unit to the building. That unit next to the restaurant will some day become my brewery, where I can blend my own special hops, but that is down the road a piece, and for now it's another shop to fill.

The heart and soul of the kitchen would be where we housed *"The Smoker Beast"*. That's right, you heard me, *"The Smoker Beast"*, beloved by all and from day one that was our affectionate name for the huge smoker, the beast that would house every piece of meat on its way to barbecue bliss. *"The Beast"*, although a gentle giant, could devour thousands of pounds of the best pecan wood, which is local to the area. Wood that I believe is the key to my secret barbecue magic! Of course we had the walk in freezers, wash basins and the all-important corner in the back, in the dark—my office—my man cave!

I left the interior design to Donna, although we worked on it together, all along the way, with daily phone calls like *"what do you think about this"* or *"how about that"*, it was Donna who went to town on the vibe for the warm feeling it has today. The combination of Donna's feel for the interior and my being at the restaurant everyday, all day—ideas had their way of working into our heads. Heck, some of my best ideas came late at night. I would be driving away and another thought would enter my filled head. Soon, the restaurant began to grow organically.

Donna's longtime collection of ideas was starting to take shape. From the ceiling we hung the old-fashioned vintage style light bulbs from long dangling black wires. The lights were minimalist, and the warm glow of the filament bulb was just what we were looking for in the design. It gave the feeling of the saloons, lit just right, so you could see the cowpoke or cowgirl next to you.

The light gave a
warm cast to the room;
all was good
with the world.

Wood became a very important part to the look of the restaurant. We wanted booths, but not too many, just a couple so that you would want to get there early and mark your spot. To this day people stake their claim to their favorite spot each week. Drawing on my love of the old west, the booths are surrounded by tall wooden sides of Alder wood, offering privacy to the booth with a rough-hewn texture, stained in a deep walnut color. The booths were strategically placed, comfy with plush leather and brass studs embedded around the outside cushions. The tabletops are thick Alder wood as well, and are tucked up against the wall with good views of the kitchen and all the guests on center stage.

Oddly enough and maybe part of life's plan, there was an incredibly talented couple who had the shop next door to us where they made furniture—you guessed it, they made every table by hand for Bryan's Black Mountain Barbecue. We used a combination of Alder wood and pine to get the effect of our old west yet modern cowboy look, melding the old with the new while retaining the western flavor. The very first thing you will see when you walk in is the immense round table centered under a wagon wheel fitted with flickering lights, as though the gas lamps are on and open for business. One thing led to another. It was the patina on the old wagon wheel that dictated the color for the walls and helped to bring in the idea of acid washed copper walls that run along the lower half of every wall, with the faint hint of a few pigs stenciled here and there. The acid left all sorts of blended Southwest colors much like the blend of all our ideas. Donna and I were the designers and the workers on that effort.

The huge round center table can seat at least 10. It shows every aspect of the Alder, and carries a finish that is richly polished. The wood grain pattern reminds me of the old leather faces of a worn cowboy that hold so many secrets of their journey.

Around the huge center table are a number of pine-topped tables all finished in a Palo Verde color bringing in the feel of the outside, where huge trees shade the patio. Again, Donna searched for just the right chairs adding an eclectic touch of raw stainless steel, circa 1934 in style, which add to the clean cowboy comfort.

The floors were already cement, which would work well when you have barbecue sauce flowing like a river. The floor was etched with grooves to make a diagonal pattern in huge sweeping diamond shapes. We painted the floors with a soothing, warm tone of deep Palo Verde Beetle.

We took a look around at the walls above the wood dado, which separated the acid washed base. We decided they needed to become red brick, bringing in the warmth to the area and the color of a deep Arizona sunset. Everyday something new was added. To give you an example, I was standing there talking to the plumbers and they said, *"How would you feel about a railing for the customer line that would be made out of iron plumbing pipe?"* I have to say that was the farthest from my mind, creative, but out there for sure. But that's the old west, ingenuity with a capital *"I"*. It worked like a charm. It had that dark warm feeling with twists and turns that would give guests a place to talk to friends as they waited in line to order.

All the walls are graced with old time western posters of my friends like Will Hart, Tom Mix, Bill Boyd and Roy Rogers. How can you miss with a team of wranglers like that watching over the homestead?

Overhead, there hangs the big screen that shows old black and white westerns all day and all night much to the delight of the customers. The guys are all there doing their best to entertain. Old west style ballads play as background to a dream that has come to life for us.

One day I called up Donna and said we need a huge neon sign for the wall, we could hang it above the long table with the benches where families could sit in a cozy corner. What barbecue joint would be complete without neon? Donna thought I was crazy. I searched all over for the best neon sign creator I could find. Little did I know that this would soon become the signature for everything we do at Bryan's Black Mountain Barbecue.

Signs are everywhere on the walls, many of which Donna has had in storage for the very day we would have our own restaurant. Everywhere we went another group of words would have meaning to her—*"Hippies Use Side Door"* hangs above the exit, *"Be Nice or Leave"* above the drink station, *"Eat"* in huge script is on the wall just behind the order window. Messages to our friends that you are finally home on the range.

As we have grown, so has our *"Wall of Fame"* photos of TV personalities, bull riders, friends and the articles that have praised all of our hard efforts. Guests love to see what you have been up to and that you have been recognized amongst your peers.

I would be totally remiss if I didn't mention my friend the old guitar that hangs on the wall with a sign *"play me"*. Pull the guitar off the wall and play a few tunes—it's all about soul. Heck, I have been known to play a few for the crowds myself.

Paul Boruff: traveling singer, song writer and guitar player.

SMOKER TIP

PROPER TEMPERATURES:

I'm never without a good quality meat thermometer. This is number one on the list for a reason. There's nothing worse than a dried out cut of meat that eats like "shoe leather". Put the "heat to the meat" and watch it carefully.

The perfect temperature for smoking your meat is:

225° – 250°

BRISKET

8-10 lbs, 12–14 hours. Remove from smoker at:

185° – 190°

PORK BUTT

8-10 lbs, 12–14 hours. Remove from smoker at:

185° – 190°

CHICKEN

3 lb whole chicken, 2 hours -
Remove from smoker at:

165°

RIBS

St. Louis Spare Ribs, 2 ½ lbs 5–6 hours - Remove from smoker when the meat begins to separate from the bone.
NOTE: It's all in the trim, ask your butcher.

Pictured above right, an Alexander Girard playing card from Braniff Airlines

(serves 2-4)
2 slabs, approx. 5 lbs
6 tbsp Bryan's Spice Rub *(page 97)*

ST. LOUIS CUT SPARE RIBS

Trim ribs of excess fat and remove any membrane.
Season both sides with Bryan's Spice Rub. Heat smoker to 225°.
When hot, add ribs and smoke for 5–6 hours, or until ribs are tender.

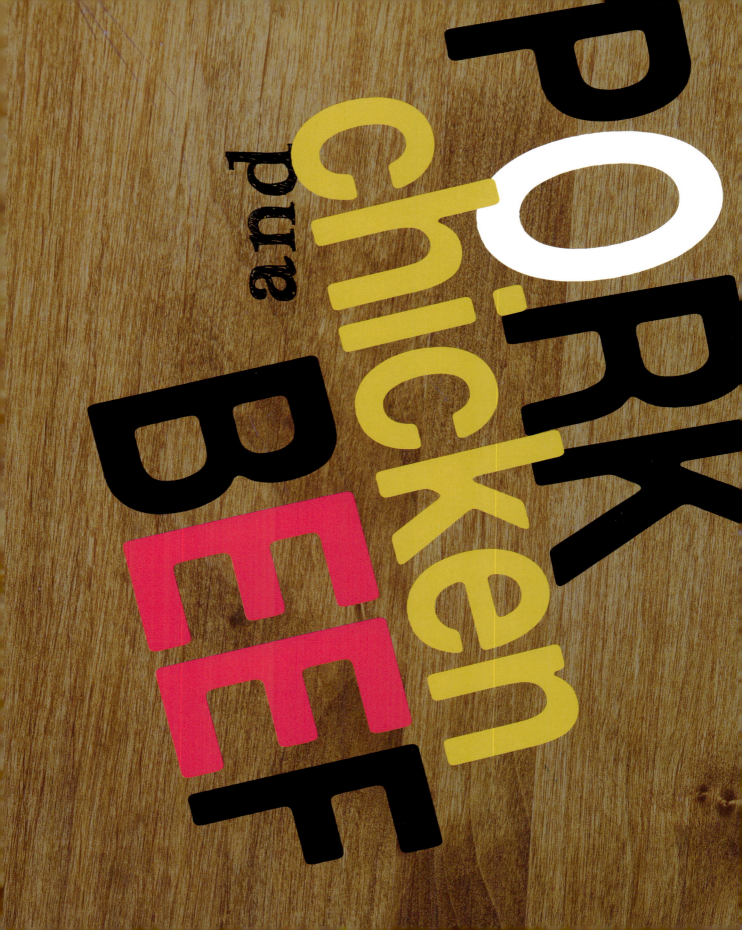

PORK
Chicken
and
BEEF

SMOKER TIP

PREPARATION:

RIBS need tender loving care before you hit the smoker or grill. Always remove the thin membrane from the back of the ribs. Start by getting a corner of the membrane loosened with the tip of your knife. Take some dry paper towel and grab the membrane corner and pull back gently. The skin will lift off as you pull back; discard membrane and you are ready to go.

CHICKEN: Be sure to clean out any of the "gnarly bits" inside the bird and wash thoroughly. Pat dry and cover with your favorite rub, Bryan's of course!

PORK BUTT: Don't worry it's not the back end like it sounds, it's actually from the shoulder which makes one heck of a good BBQ. When you buy a Pork Butt or Shoulder, as it is known, there is little preparation. Check to be sure there is a nice fat cap and I prefer it with the bone-in. It naturally has a perfect amount of fat for BBQ and it's always juicy and moist. Have at it; give that pork a good seasoned rub.

CREEKER RIBS with PRICKLY PEAR LIME BBQ SAUCE

RIBS

(serves 2–4)

2 slabs St. Louis spare ribs

6 tbsp Bryan's Spice Rub *(page 97)*

PRICKLY PEAR LIME BBQ SAUCE

(makes 15 cups)

5 cups tomato sauce

5 cups ketchup

4 ½ cups prickly pear syrup

½ cup raspberry vinegar

½ cup lime juice

½ tbsp crushed coriander seed

¼ tbsp coarse black pepper

½ tsp granulated garlic

1 ½ tbsp Kosher salt

1 tbsp chili powder

RIBS Trim ribs of excess fat and remove any membrane. Season both sides with Bryan's Spice Rub. Heat smoker to 225°. When hot, add ribs and smoke for 5–6 hours, or until ribs are tender.

SAUCE Add all ingredients to a large pot and simmer until thickened. Cool and pour into jars or plastic containers. Seal and store in the refrigerator.

SMOKED SAUSAGE SANDWICH
with PICKLED WATERMELON RIND CHOW CHOW

SANDWICH

4 French rolls

4 each pork sausage, uncooked

8 oz Pickled Watermelon Rind Chow Chow

4 oz Bryan's BBQ Sauce *(page 96)*

PICKLED WATERMELON RIND

4 lbs watermelon rind – green and
 red removed

2 tbsp allspice

2 tbsp whole cloves

1 quart water

1 quart cider vinegar

3 ½ lbs sugar

½ tsp mustard seed

CHOW CHOW

2 ½ cups cider vinegar

1 ½ cups sugar

3 tsp dry mustard

2 tsp ground turmeric

½ tsp ground ginger

2 tsp celery seed

4 tsp mustard seed

2 cups chopped celery

2 cups chopped red onion

2 cups chopped bell pepper

1 cup yellow mustard

2 cups Pickled Watermelon Rind

SANDWICH Smoke sausage in smoker for approximately 1 hour or until internal temperature is 165° and reserve for serving. Slice roll lengthwise, toast in pan or on griddle with butter. Place sausage on toasted bun, top with 2 oz of chow chow and 1 oz Bryan's BBQ Sauce.

PICKLED WATERMELON RIND Peel the green skin off the rind and cut off inner pink watermelon rind. You will be left with the white rind and it's going to get happy.

Combine allspice, cloves, mustard seed, cider vinegar, water and sugar. Heat until sugar dissolves.

Add watermelon rind and simmer 45 minutes to 1 hour. Rind will look translucent but still have some bite to it.

Remove from heat and cool overnight in the *"brine"*.

Dice into small chunks.

CHOW CHOW Add vinegar, sugar, dry mustard, turmeric, ginger, celery seed and mustard seed in a small saucepan. Slowly heat, and simmer about 10 minutes. Add celery, onion and bell pepper. Simmer another 10 minutes.

Remove from heat and add mustard. Stir and place in a covered container. Keep in refrigerator.

Combine Chow Chow with 2 cups pickled Watermelon Rind. Serve cold or room temperature.

"This is a little tricky and takes a bit of time but you are going to love this one—the results are amazing."

BRYAN'S BIG ONE

Toasted bun
4 oz French fries
4 oz pulled pork
2 oz Bryan's BBQ Sauce *(page 96)*
1 oz sliced Sweet Pickled Jalapeño *(page 78)*
4 oz cole slaw
1 fried egg

CONSTRUCTION NOTES

This is a layering process—inch by inch. Start with the bottom toasted bun, pile on the fries, then the pulled pork, sauce the pork. Top all of that with the sliced Sweet Pickled Jalapeño, cole slaw, fried egg and then the bun.

BUN

FRIED EGG

COLE SLAW

SWEET PICKLED JALAPEÑO

BRYAN'S BBQ SAUCE

PULLED PORK

FRIES

BUN

PORK BUTT

(serves 20)

8–10 lbs pork butt
4 tbsp Bryan's Spice Rub *(page 97)*

Trim pork butt of excess fat. Season meat, skipping fat side with Bryan's Spice Rub. Heat the smoker to 225°, and when hot add pork.

Smoke for about 12–14 hours or until pork reaches an internal temperature of 185°–190°. Cool slightly, and while still warm, use hands to pull apart.

PULLED PORK SANDWICH

Pull the pork and place on bun.
Top with Bryan's BBQ Sauce. *(page 96)*

Be daring. Top with cole slaw.

FIREBIRD CHICKEN (The Chicken From Hell)

CHICKEN
(serves 2)
1 whole chicken, cut in half
½ oz Bryan's Spice Rub *(page 97)*

GLAZE
(makes 3 cups)
8 oz Bryan's BBQ Sauce *(page 96)*
Zest and juice of 1 orange
12 oz honey
8 ea habanero peppers*
  (6 for the glaze, 2 for garnish)
1 oz chopped fresh ginger

GARNISH
2 habaneros sliced in rings
1 oz scallions sliced thinly

CHICKEN Season chicken with rub and place in a smoker, 1 1/2 to 2 hours until chicken reaches internal temperature of 165°.

GLAZE Combine all ingredients (except for 2 of the habaneros) and blend in food processor. Pour into small sauce pan and cook until mixture thickens (careful not to burn) for approximately 5–10 minutes.

PLATE Place the hot chicken halves on slices of fresh bread and spoon over glaze. Garnish with scallions and sliced habaneros.

* **WARNING!** *Wear gloves when handling habanero peppers—don't touch anything!*

BRYAN'S BARBECUE CHICKEN

(serves 2)

1 large chicken, about 3 lbs halved
2-3 tbsp Bryan's Spice Rub *(page 97)*

Heat smoker to 225°–250°. If whole, cut chicken in half. Coat chicken with Spice Rub and place in smoker. Cook for 1 1/2 to 2 hours, or until internal temperature of the bird reaches 165° and the juices run clear. Remove from smoker and allow to rest 5 minutes before serving.

Add a good blanket of Bryan's BBQ Sauce, serve over 2 slices of good old fashioned white bread—it's a barbecue tradition.

PULLED CHICKEN SANDWICH

Remove skin, pull the chicken apart, shredding by hand and place on bun. Top with Bryan's BBQ Sauce. *(page 96)*

Why did the chicken cross the road? (answer on page 99)

SPRING CHICKEN SALAD SANDWICH

SPRING CHICKEN SALAD

1 lb smoked chicken chilled and diced
2 oz asparagus sliced
2 oz baby carrots sliced
2 oz peas
1 oz red onion diced
½ tsp thyme
½ cup Molasses Dijon Spread
1 cup mayo
1 tsp honey
Salt and black pepper to taste

Combine all ingredients and chill, serve on toasted buns.

MOLASSES DIJON SPREAD

(makes 3 cups)

2 cups mayonnaise
1 cup Dijon mustard
½ tbsp molasses
1 tsp Kosher salt

Add ingredients to a large mixing bowl. Using a whisk, mix until completely blended. Store covered in the refrigerator.

BEEF BRISKET

Beef Brisket 8–10 lbs
4 tbsp Bryan's Spice Rub *(page 97)*

Heat smoker to 225° to 250°. Wash and trim brisket, leaving a good fat cap. Season well with Bryan's Spice Rub. (no need to season the fatty side).

Place meat in smoker, fat side up, for 12–14 hrs at 225° to 250°. Remove meat when it reaches approx. 190°.

BRISKET SANDWICH

Slice brisket and arrange on bun.
Top with Bryan's BBQ Sauce. *(page 96)*

SMOKER TIP Brisket is one of the most challenging pieces to do right but has a big payoff. You want to trim some of the fat, but not everything, the fat helps keep it moist. Season it well and watch it like a baby. This will take you about 12–14 hours depending on the size of the Brisket. Look for a brisket that is 8–10 lbs.

BRISKET BURNT END GRILLED CHEESE SANDWICH

2 slices white bread
1 oz butter
4 oz brisket burnt ends *(page 61)*
4 slices white cheddar cheese
1 oz grilled onions
1 oz Bryan's BBQ Sauce *(page 96)*

Grill bread with butter in large sauté pan.
Top bread with cheese and then brisket and onions.
When cheese is melted add Bryan's BBQ Sauce
and press two sides of sandwich together.

""*Genesis Rarebit* "Written by Bryan Dooley, 2008

I wish the Earth was big and flat like a slice of bread and that was that.
I wish the moon was made of cheese like a blue veined Stilton above the trees.

And if the sun would cooperate, the possibilities could be quite great.

Melt the cheese upon the bread as I lay asleep in my bed.
And in the morning when I awoke I'd see the Earth the cheese did cloak.

A rich new land, a brand new start to free our minds and fill our hearts.
A gentle warmer place to be and a lovely world for you and me.

PEPITA BISON BURGER topped with FIRE ROASTED POBLANO and SHIITAKE MUSHROOMS

TOPPING Get the grill ready on medium high for the topping. When hot, add peppers and grill, turning frequently, until skin blackens.

Remove peppers from grill and seal in paper bag for about 10 minutes. Remove from bag, peel blackened skin *(don't run these under water or you will loose all the flavor)* and cut into thin strips.

Next, heat large sauté pan on medium high. When hot, add oil. Slide in the mushrooms and onions to hot oil and sauté for 3 to 5 minutes, or until mushrooms are soft. Season with salt and pepper, and keep warm while grilling burgers.

BURGER Mix bison, Bryan's Spice Rub and pepitas in a bowl. Shape into 4 large patties. Brush with olive oil and place on the grill. Cook for about 5 minutes a side. Remove and top with peppers and mushroom-onion mix. Slather on some Bryan's BBQ Sauce. Serve on your favorite buns.

TOPPING
2 poblano peppers
1 tsp olive oil
2 large shiitake mushrooms
  (cut in thin strips)
1 medium red onion
  (cut in thin strips)
Salt and pepper, to taste

BURGER
2 lbs ground bison
2 tbsp Bryan's Spice Rub *(page 97)*
½ cup toasted pepitas *(pumpkin seeds)*
Olive oil for brushing
4 hamburger buns

BISON and LAMB

SAGE and JUNIPER RUBBED BISON RIBS
with a SWEET PERSIMMON GLAZE

SAGE JUNIPER RUB

2 tbsp ground juniper berries

  (a coffee grinder works well)

3 tbsp salt

1 tbsp coarse black pepper

2 tbsp ground sage

½ tbsp garlic powder

3 tbsp sugar

4 tbsp chili powder

BISON RIBS

(serves 4)

2 large racks bison ribs,

  membranes removed

SWEET PERSIMMON GLAZE

½ cup persimmon purée*

½ cup honey

2 tbsp lemon juice

RUB Place all ingredients in a mixing bowl and mix until completely blended. Pour into a spice jar and cover. Store in a dark cool place until ready to use.

GLAZE Place all ingredients in a saucepan, blend well and simmer. Keep warm until just before serving.

RIBS Prepare ribs by seasoning with 4 to 5 tablespoons of Sage and Juniper Rub. Place ribs in a 225° smoker for about 4 to 5 hours, or until ribs are tender. Remove and slather with warm persimmon glaze.

* www.localharvest.org

LAMB DRUMSTICK with GINGER BEER BBQ SAUCE

LAMB SHANKS
(serves 4)

4 lamb shanks, about 1 lb each
¼ cup Bryan's Spice Rub *(page 97)*

GINGER BEER BBQ SAUCE

3 beers, 12 oz each
2 ½ cups sugar
4 cups Bryan's BBQ Sauce *(page 96)*
2 tbsp fresh ginger, sliced in thin strips
1 tsp lemon juice
⅛ tsp cardamom
⅛ tsp allspice
2 bay leaves

LAMB SHANKS

Heat grill on medium-high heat. Season lamb with Bryan's Spice Rub. When grill is hot, place shanks away from hot coals. Cover and grill indirectly until tender, about 1 1/2 hours. Or cook in smoker at 225˚ to 250˚ for about 5 hours, or until shanks are tender. Remove from heat and slather with Ginger Beer BBQ Sauce and let the party begin! Serve immediately.

GINGER BEER BBQ SAUCE

Combine beer and sugar in a large saucepan. Heat on medium-low and simmer until reduced by half, stirring occasionally—get a beer for yourself, makes the cooking time go faster or so it seems!

Add barbecue sauce, ginger, lemon juice, cardamom, allspice and bay leaves. Continue to simmer until sauce thickens, about 20 minutes. Remove bay leaves and keep the sauce warm.

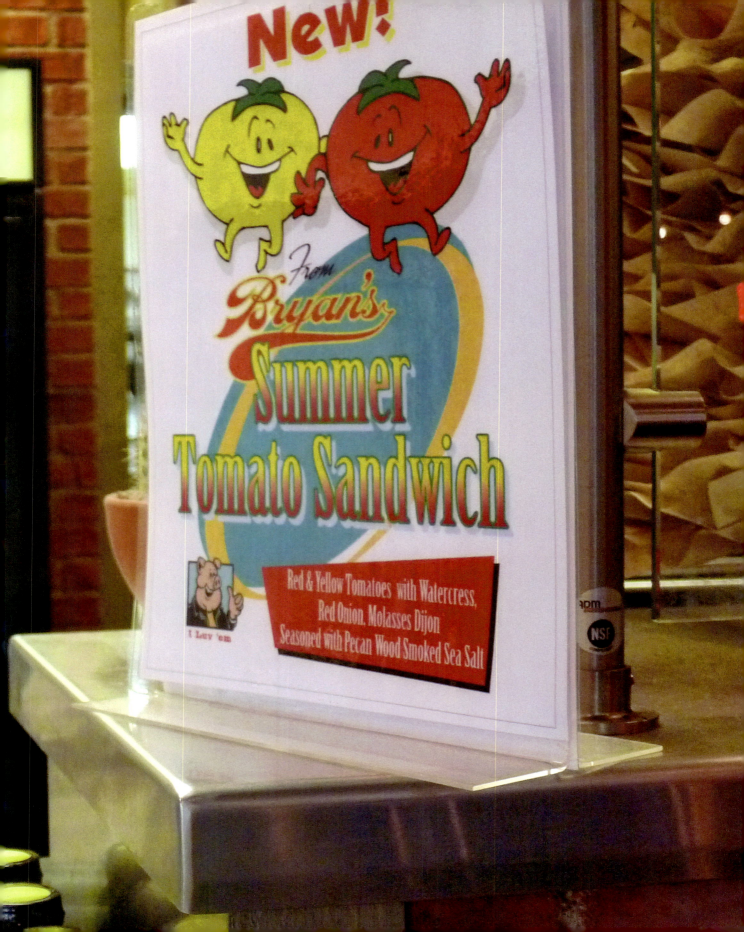

PULLED SQUASH SANDWICH

(serves 4)
1 large spaghetti squash
Water
4 oz Bryan's BBQ Sauce

Heat oven to 350°. Cut squash in half lengthwise. Remove the seeds. Place squash halves, cut side down, on a baking sheet with rim or use shallow pan.

Add a thin layer of water to the pan and bake for about 40 minutes, or until squash is completely cooked. Scoop out the squash and sauté in butter. Mix with Bryan's BBQ Sauce until heated. Serve on toasted bun.

TOP THIS SANDWICH WITH A FRIED EGG. "IT WILL MAKE YOUR EYES BUG OUT AND PUT A SMILE ON YOUR FACE."

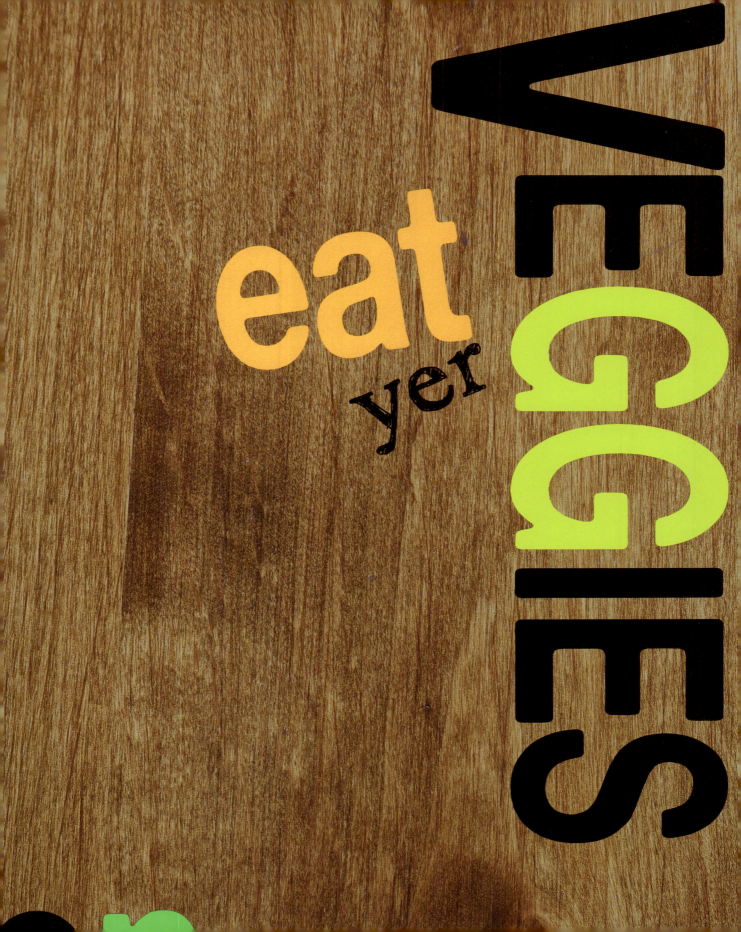

SUMMER TOMATO SANDWICH with MOLASSES DIJON SPREAD

TOMATO SANDWICH

(serves 2)
4 tbsp butter
4 slices bread
Smoked sea salt to taste *(page 96)*
2 tbsp Molasses Dijon Spread
8 slices red tomato
4 slices yellow tomato
Red onion, sliced thinly *(2 slices)*
Small bunch of watercress

MOLASSES DIJON SPREAD

(makes 3 cups)
2 cups mayonnaise
1 cup Dijon mustard
2 tbsp molasses
1 tsp Kosher salt

SANDWICH Heat sauté pan on medium heat. Add butter, and when melted, add bread and grill until both sides are toasted.

Remove from pan and spread each side of bread with equal amounts of Molasses Dijon Spread.

For each sandwich, layer 2 slices of red tomato on 1 slice of bread. Season with sea salt. Add two slices yellow tomato and season with sea salt. Add onion, 2 remaining slices of red tomato and watercress. Top with other slice of bread. Serve immediately.

SPREAD Add ingredients to a large mixing bowl. Using a whisk, mix until completely blended. Store covered in the refrigerator.

FRIED ARTICHOKE PO'BOY
with SMOKED TOMATO REMOULADE

(serves 2)

2 cups rice flour

2 tbsp Bryan's Spice Rub *(page 97)*

**10 oz canned and quartered
    artichoke hearts, drained**

Vegetable oil for frying

2 French rolls

Butter to taste

¼ cup Smoked Tomato Remoulade

¼ cup shredded Romaine lettuce

¼ cup diced tomato

SMOKED TOMATO REMOULADE

(serves 6)

1 lb ripe tomatoes, peeled and smoked

1 cup diced red onion

¼ cup Sweet Pickled Jalapeños *(page 78)*

3 cups mayonnaise

¼ cup yellow mustard

2 tbsp lemon juice

2 tbsp Worcestershire sauce

Mix rice flour and spice together in a large mixing bowl. Dredge artichoke hearts in flour mixture, coating all sides. Fill a deep pot with 3 or 4 inches of vegetable oil. Heat on medium-high heat. When hot, gently add artichoke hearts in batches, and fry until crispy, about 5 minutes.

Remove hearts and keep warm while assembling sandwich. Split the rolls in half lengthwise and butter to taste. Gently toast on a grill or in a frying pan, about 2 minutes. Spread remoulade on both sides of roll. Add fried artichoke hearts. Top with lettuce and tomato. Serve immediately.

REMOULADE Bring a pot of water to a boil. Add tomatoes in small batches, and blanch about 1–2 minutes.

Remove and place in a bowl of ice water. When cool, peel and cut each tomato into 6 equal pieces. Smoke about 45 minutes to 1 hour. Remove and cool.

Next, place tomatoes, red onion and jalapeños in a food processor and pulse into the consistency of relish. Strain mixture to remove the liquid. Discard liquid. In a large mixing bowl, combine mayonnaise, mustard, lemon juice and Worcestershire sauce. Whisk until well blended. Fold in tomato mixture and mix until blended.

"It all came together in my head right away for the sandwich. A Remoulade is what you would put on a Po'Boy anyway, but for the BBQ twist I wanted to bring in the flavor by smoking the tomato. I like to go back and forth with my Sous Chef Rob and see his thoughts and this is what we came up with, enjoy!"

SWEET PICKLED JALAPEÑOS

10 lbs fresh jalapeños
1 ¾ gallons cider vinegar
4 lbs sugar
½ lb Kosher salt
½ lb garlic cloves, peeled
1 tbsp dried thyme
3 cinnamon sticks
1 ½ tbsp whole celery seed
3 tbsp mustard seed
1 ¾ lb red onions, peeled and sliced

Wash jalapeños and pierce with knife and reserve.

To make brine, place all ingredients except jalapeños in a large, non-reactive, stainless or enamel saucepan. Bring to a boil over high heat. When boiling, reduce heat to medium low, and stir briefly to dissolve sugar and spices.

Add half of the raw jalapeños to brine. Simmer about 10–15 minutes until skins start to wrinkle. Use slotted spoon to remove jalapeños and place in a large container.

Next, add the remaining jalapeños and simmer about 10–15 minutes. Remove to container.

Pour warm brine over jalapeños and allow to cool. Store jalapeños in covered jars. Refrigerate.

"It's six pack for a reason! There's a six pack in every batch at Bryan's."

SIX PACK COWBOY BEANS

COWBOY BEANS
(serves 8-10)
½ cup diced celery
½ cup diced red onion
½ cup diced green bell pepper
4 oz diced smoked sausage
1 clove minced garlic
Olive oil as needed
1 ea beer
¼ cup yellow mustard
½ cup molasses
1 cup Bryan's BBQ Sauce *(page 96)*
2 tbsp chili powder
4 ea 15 oz cans of cooked white beans,
drained and rinsed

Add a little olive oil to medium pot.
Add celery, onions, and bell pepper.
Cook until vegetables begin to soften.
Next, sauté garlic and sausage in mixture.
Then add beer and simmer for a couple
minutes to cook off alcohol. Add
remaining ingredients and simmer
until sauce thickens.

"Barley, Hops, Water and Yeast" Written by Bryan Dooley, 2008

Barley, Hops,
Water and Yeast,
You know that's all
we really need.
Barley, Hops,
Water and Yeast,
Let's go make some Beer!

Beer, Beer,
make some Beer.
Beer, Beer,
make some Beer,
Beer, Beer,
make some Beer,
Let's go make some Beer.

Barley, Hops,
Water and Yeast,
Barley, Hops,
Water and Yeast,
Barley, Hops,
Water and Yeast,
Let's go make some Beer.

Barley, Hops,
Water and Yeast,
You know that's all
we really need.
Barley, Hops,
Water and Yeast,
Let's go make some Beer!

Beer, Beer,
make some Beer.
Beer, Beer,
make some Beer,
Beer, Beer,
make some Beer,
Let's go make some Beer!

Barley, Hops,
Water and Yeast,
Barley, Hops,
Water and Yeast,
Barley, Hops,
Water and Yeast,
Let's go make some Beer.

BAKED POTATO SALAD

"This is my absolute favorite side dish. It's really familiar but it makes all the twists and turns I like when creating my own take on a classic. Baking the potato adds that secret turn, and with a dash of herbs it really sparks the fresh and bold flavors."

(serves 6-8)

6 each Russet potatoes
Olive oil as needed
½ cup sliced green onions
1 ½ cups sour cream
½ cup mayonnaise
2 tsp dried dill
Salt and pepper to taste

Heat oven to 350°

Wash and dry potatoes, rub lightly with olive oil and bake about 45 minutes, or until potatoes are fully cooked.

While baking, mix sour cream, mayonnaise, scallions and dill in a mixing bowl. Cover and refrigerate until ready to toss the salad.

Remove potatoes when done, and allow to cool. Next, dice into bite size pieces and place in a large mixing bowl. Gently mix potatoes with dressing, salt and pepper to taste. Cool in the refrigerator at least an hour before serving.

CRAWFISH MAC and CHEESE

1 qt cream
½ onion
2 whole cloves
1 bay leaf
Pinch of nutmeg
2 oz Roux
7 oz white cheddar, shredded
7 oz Gruyère, shredded
1 lb package of elbow macaroni
1 lb crawfish tails *

Combine cream, onion, cloves, bay leaf and a pinch of nutmeg and bring to simmer. Whisk in Roux and cook for about 20 minutes. At a simmer it should be smooth, strain to remove onion, bay leaf, cloves and return to simmer. Add in cheeses.

Cook macaroni according to package directions. Begin sautéing crawfish tails to heat through. Combine cheese sauce to the cooked macaroni and crawfish. Ready to eat.

* www.lacrawfish.com

ROB'S COLLARD GREENS

½ lb pulled pork
Meat from 1 slab smoked ribs
   with bones reserved, about 10 oz
3 bunches collard greens, washed,
   trimmed and cut—about 1 lb cleaned
1 large onion chopped 8–10 oz
3 cloves garlic chopped
3 tbsp canola oil
3 qt chicken stock
Bryan's Spice Rub as needed *(page 97)*
Tabasco as needed

Sweat the onions and garlic in oil, season. Deglaze the pan with one bottle (12 oz) of favorite beer. Add meat and stock and bring to a boil. Add greens and reduce, heat to a simmer, for 45 minutes to an hour until tender. Adjust the seasoning to taste and add Tabasco. *(optional)*

FARMER'S SALAD

(serves 8)
2 cups cauliflower florets
2 cups European cucumbers, sliced
¾ cup diced red onion
¾ cup diced red bell pepper
¾ cup frozen peas
2 ½ cups sour cream
¼ cup red wine vinegar
1 tbsp dried dill
1 tbsp Kosher salt
½ tsp black pepper

Add cauliflower, cucumbers, red onion, red bell pepper and peas in a large mixing bowl. In a separate bowl, add sour cream, red wine vinegar, dill, salt and pepper. Mix well.

Blend sour cream dressing with vegetables.

Serve immediately.

OLIVE COLE SLAW
for a CROWD

DRESSING

4 cups mayonnaise

1 cup cider vinegar

1 cup sugar

1 tsp dried thyme leaves

2 tbsp Old Bay Seasoning

Add ingredients into a large mixing bowl. Use a whisk to blend completely.

OLIVE COLE SLAW

(serves 20)

5 lbs cabbage, shredded

½ lb julienne carrots

6 oz julienne Kalamata olives

8 oz julienne green olives

Dress coleslaw to taste. Cover and chill.

BRYAN'S CARDAMOM SNICKERDOODLE ICE CREAM SANDWICH

COOKIE

(Makes 2 dozen large cookies)

2 ¾ cups all purpose flour
1 ½ cups sugar
2 tsp cream of tartar
1 tsp baking soda
½ tsp salt
1 cup butter softened
2 large eggs
1 tsp vanilla

Preheat oven to 400°

In a large bowl mix together the flour, salt, baking powder and cream of tartar.

In your mixer bowl, beat the butter and sugar until smooth. Add the eggs and vanilla, scrape down the sides of the bowl. Add the flour mixture and beat until the dough is smooth. Dough needs to be firm so you may need to refrigerate.

Shape the dough into round balls, roll into coating and place on parchment lined baking sheets.

Bake the cookies for about 8–10 minutes, or until they are nicely golden brown.

SUGAR COATING

¼ cup sugar
2 tsp cardamom

Any type of ice cream that you like would go great in between these cookies. What I like to do is take a good vanilla ice cream, about a gallon should do. Soften it and mix in fresh raspberries and blackberries. Re-chill your mixture. Place a scoop between the two cookies and you will have one *"kick-ass"* ice cream sandwich. As an added bonus, soak additional berries in a nice hoppy IPA Beer and spoon the juices and berries around the sandwich.

just DESSERTS

ROOT BEER BATTERED APPLES

(serves 4)

2–3 medium sized apples

1 egg

1 cup cold root beer

1 cup flour

    (use rice flour if staying Gluten Free)

As needed powdered sugar

As needed pink peppercorns

In a medium saucepan, heat 3–4 inches of oil. In mixing bowl beat the egg. Add cold root beer and flour, mix together lightly.

Peel and core apples and slice in 1/4 inch rings. Dip apples in batter and fry in oil until golden brown.

Dust with powdered sugar and whole pink peppercorns to taste.

WATERMELON WEDGES
with CARDAMOM HONEY

(serves 6)
6 slices of watermelon
3 tbsp cardamom honey
1 jalapeño, seeds removed and diced
into small pieces

CARDAMOM HONEY
1 cup honey
½ tsp ground cardamom

Take one cup of honey, warmed.
Stir in 1/2 tsp ground cardamom.

WATERMELON Chill one watermelon.

Cut the watermelon into quarter sized wedges,
drizzle the honey and cardamom over the
chilled slices. Garnish with diced jalapeño.

Dice the jalapeños being sure to remove all
membrane and seeds. This will ensure that
the jalapeños are not too hot as the garnish

I like to serve the wedges on a platter
for guests, drizzle all slices and garnish. .

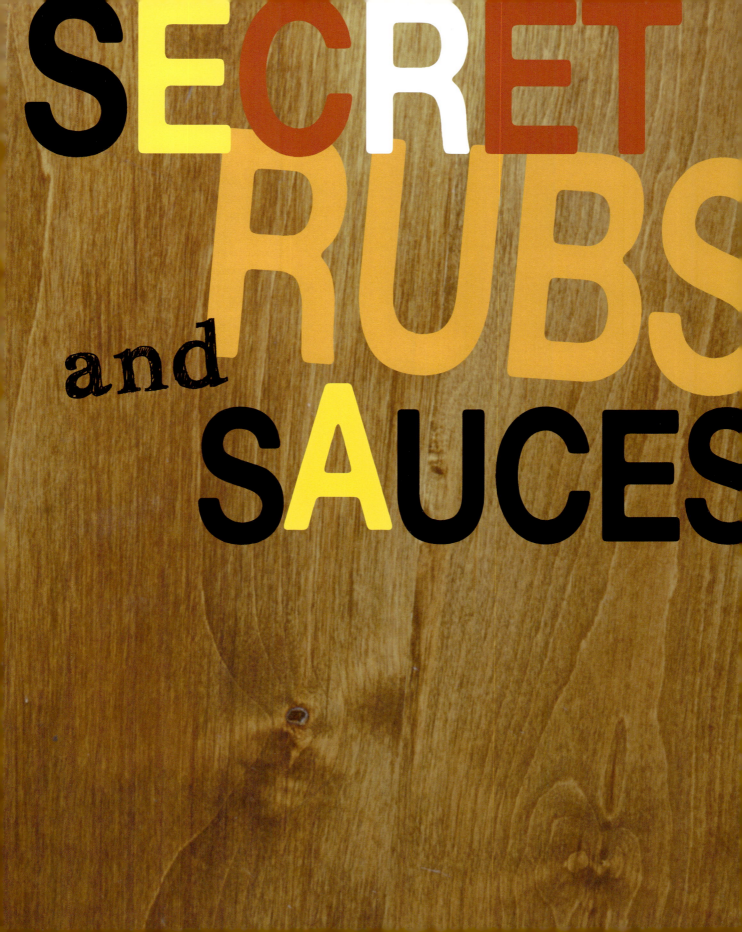

SECRET RUBS and SAUCES

Almost
BRYAN'S BBQ SAUCE
"Sort of, well I can't tell all my secrets."

32 oz ketchup
32 oz tomato sauce
12 oz cider vinegar
2 oz honey
½ cup brown sugar
12 oz beer
1 tbsp crushed red pepper
2 tbsp chili powder
1 tsp granulated garlic
1 tsp coarse black pepper
2 tbsp lemon juice
2 ea bay leaves

Combine all ingredients in sauce pan.
Simmer for approx 20 minutes or until
sauce thickens. Remove bay leaves.

Firebird Glaze 22
Lemon Pepper Vinaigrette 27
Prickly Pear Lime BBQ Sauce 49
Pickled Watermelon Rind 51
Chow Chow 51
Molasses Dijon Spread 60
Fire Roasted Poblano and Shiitake Mushrooms 64
Sage and Juniper Rub 66
Sweet Persimmon Glaze 66
Ginger Beer BBQ Sauce 69
Smoked Tomato Remoulade 77

SMOKED SALT   1 lb Fleur de Sel

Spread salt evenly on a flat sheet pan. Smoke for about 12
hours in smoker, stirring occasionally. Once cooled, store in
an airtight container in a cool, dark cupboard.

Nearly
BRYAN'S SPICE RUB

6 tbsp salt

6 tbsp chili powder

4 tbsp paprika

2 tbsp course black pepper

2 tbsp sugar

1 tsp dry thyme

1 tsp ground celery seed

1 tbsp granulated garlic

2 tsp dry oregano

4 tsp allspice

Combine all ingredients.

SMOKER TIP **A Good Rub:** Here's where you can excel in your creativity. There are the basic flavors for many of the rubs but don't forget about what works best with the meat you are preparing such as Bison. Bison roam freely grazing among juniper and sage, so that's a natural flavor for your bison ribs. Other great rub ingredients include: brown sugar, smoked salt, red pepper, paprika, chili powder, celery seed, allspice—let your creative juices run wild. Make sure your spice rub has a good balance of salt, sweet and spices.

BRYAN'S BBQ PANTRY

BREADS
Burger Buns
French Rolls

CANNED GOODS
Artichoke Hearts
Black-Eyed Peas
Tomato Sauce
Whole Tomatoes

CONDIMENTS
Dijon Mustard
Honey
Ketchup
Mayonnaise
Molasses
Worcestershire
Yellow Mustard

DAIRY & EGGS
Butter
Buttermilk
Eggs
Gruyère
Sour Cream
White Cheddar

DRIED HERBS & SPICES
Allspice
Bay Leaves
Bryan's Rub
Cardamom
Celery Seed
Chipotle Pepper Powder
Cinnamon Sticks
Cloves
Coarse Black Pepper
Coriander Powder
Coriander Seeds
Cumin
Dill
Dry Mustard
Garlic Powder
Ginger, Powdered
Granulated Garlic
Ground Mace
Ground Nutmeg
Ground Pepper
Ground Turmeric
Juniper Berries

Kosher Salt
Mustard Seeds
Old Bay Seasoning
Oregano
Parsley Flakes
Pink Peppercorns
Rubbed Sage
Sea Salt
Smoked Salt
Smokey Paprika
Thyme
Turmeric Ground

DRY GOODS
Brown Sugar
Corn Meal
Elbow Macaroni
Rice Flour
Pepitas
Powdered Sugar

MEATS
Beef Brisket
Bison Ribs
Cabrito (Goat)
Chicken
Crawfish Tails
Lamb Shanks
Pork Butt
Pork Ribs
Pork Sausage
Shrimp
Wing Drumettes

MISC.
Baking Powder
Baking Soda
Chicken Stock
Cream of Tartar
Green Olives
Kalamata Olives
Persimmon Purée
Prickly Pear Syrup
Vanilla

OIL
Olive Oil
Canola Oil
Vegetable Oil

PRODUCE
Apples
Asparagus
Bell Pepper
Carrots
Cauliflower
Celery
Cloves
Collard Greens
Cucumber
Garlic
Fingerling Potatoes
Fresh Berries
Fresh Ginger
Frozen Corn
Frozen Lima Beans
Frozen Peas
Habaneros
Jalapeños
Lemons
Lime
Mint
Onion
Oranges
Pepitas (Pumpkin Seeds)
Poblano Peppers
Red Onions
Red Pepper
Romaine Lettuce
Russet Potatoes
Scallions
Shiitake Mushrooms
Spaghetti Squash
Tomatoes
Watercress
Watermelon

SPIRITS & BEVERAGES
Beer
Root Beer

VINEGAR
Cider Vinegar
Raspberry Vinegar
Red Wine Vinegar
White Vinegar

WOODS
Apple
Cherry
Hickory
Mesquite
Pecan

POTATO   YUKON GOLD/FINGE...

LIMA BEANS ✓

BUTTER ✓

S + P / BBM BBQ RU...

CAYENNE / HOT SAUCE...

STOCK ✓

WORCESTERSHIR... ✓

CIDER VIN...

ONION ✓

2 GOAT ?

4 CHICKENS

3 GAL STOCK

2 #10 CANS TO...
CRUSHED

(answer from page 60)
He saw Bryan's grocery list.

Wood is totally a personal preference although certain woods lend themselves to some meats better than others. My personal preference is for fruit and nut woods such as Pecan, Hickory, Oak, Apple, Pear, Peach, Cherry. In the restaurant we use Pecan wood because it gives off a softer smoke which allows me to smoke for a longer period of time without overpowering the natural meat flavor. If I use Hickory I tend to blend it with other woods such as apple. Mesquite is a traditional wood for Texas Brisket but it can be overpowering because it gives off a very intense smoke.

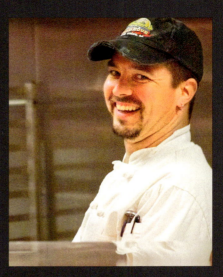

ROB OLSON
Sous Chef

2 Years at Bryan's Barbecue

Indiana University of PA,
Academy of Culinary Arts

**Hobbies are photography, music,
outdoor anything and reading**

Favorite Authors are
Robert Jordan and Stephen King

ADRIA PENTKOWSKI
Manager

2.5 Years at Bryan's Barbecue

Hobbies are hiking, long walks
with my dogs and I love movies

Favorite Author is Jean Auel

What's the one thing that draws you to Bryan's Barbecue? It's the food, the people a combination of things here. Being recognized as one of the best in the Valley and you don't have to be fussy about silverware and linens. Just being able to make a good product people love.

If you could work with one person for the dinner rush, who would it be - living or dead and what would their job be? Anthony Bourdain, color commentary for the evening.

Too tired to cook – what do you pick up? Reuben from JJ's Deli in Scottsdale, East Coast Rules!

Favorite kitchen smell? Garlic and Olive Oil Sauté.

A person walks into the restaurant and they are a famous "someone" to add to the photo "Wall of Fame" who's photo are you taking for the wall? Of course - Anthony Bourdain

Leno, Letterman, Fallen, Kimmel or O'Brien: Letterman

Favorite band? Stones and Led Zeppelin

Dinner for eight – you are sitting too, who are the other six and what is served? Jimmy Hendrix, Janis Joplin, Jon Bonham, John Belushi and Elvis **Served:** Comfort Foods - Chicken Pot Pies, Collard Greens, Fried PB and Banana Sandwiches and Chocolate Pudding.

You are the Chef for the evening at the White House you pick the year and who is your favorite attendee? 1962, Marilyn Monroe **What's their favorite dish you served?** Lobster Bisque

What's the one thing you haven't accomplished that you would like to? I'll know it after I do it.

What's the one thing that draws you to Bryan's Barbecue? I really enjoy the banter with the customers, I love giving them a hard time and seeing the regulars.

If you could work with one person for the dinner rush, who would it be - living or dead and what would their job be? In no way do I mean to sound conceited, but... ME!!! I am to some, annoyingly, all over the place tending to the needs of others. **Job:** Assistant

Too tired to cook – what do you pick up? Chinese

Favorite kitchen smell? Sautéed onions.

A person walks into the restaurant and they are a famous "someone" to add to the photo "Wall of Fame" who's photo are you taking for the wall? Wallace and Ladmo, they were childhood fixtures in the Valley and I loved them.

Leno, Letterman, Fallen, Kimmel or O'Brien: Fallen

Favorite band? Stones

Dinner for eight – you are sitting too, who are the other six and what is served? We'll be having a potluck dinner with my father, Jim, my mother, Marilyn, John Wayne (Dad loved The Duke), Alan Alda (he always made Mom laugh), my lifelong friend, Jean (she makes me laugh, AND she's an amazing cook!), and Jesus Christ (I say his name enough; I should probably meet the man)...

What's the one thing you haven't accomplished that you would like to? Get over the fear of working out in a gym!

Let's step outside for a minute, too. What we liked so much about the location is the cozy front patio area. Huge Palo Verde trees surround the patio with all of the natural dessert flowing around it—rugged boulders, Staghorn Cactus, Cholla, Prickly Pear and the sounds of the Cactus Wrens happy to see a new neighbor. We tried to really keep the area as organic as possible, so around the patio we built railing that could be drenched in the summer monsoon rains, rusting to a warm patina.

The center of the patio is our landmark, a huge, hundred plus year old Saguaro cactus towering over the patio. From the moment we saw the Saguaro we knew this was destined for a round bar that would become the town gathering place, like the old west where you gathered around the campfire. This area would

have to wait until we could get the restaurant up and running. The patio was a must have, so that guests would be able sit and take in our incredible weather, weather that the winter visitors dream of as they are shoveling feet of snow.

The patio has swinging gates, so you can saunter up to the front and come in for some of the best barbecue you will ever taste, or so I am told!

You can't help but wonder about this little town of Cave Creek

as you drive on through. It's almost as though time stood still in some ways and yet there are all the signs of hidden gems, behind what appears to be rickety wooden doors, old corrals and dusty places to park—be it your car or your horse!

Heading to the west down Cave Creek Road you will see there's bull-riding events, located at the Buffalo Chip Saloon, just west of Harold's Cave Creek Corral, both old time dining spots that still entertain the wranglers. Many a time you will see the locals ride up on their favorite steed and tie up before heading in for exceptional *"Good Eats"* or just to hang out with their friends.

Don't let the spurs and chaps throw you because behind those old doors are a host of celebrated artists, writers, well-known chefs and just plain town folk who love the Southwest.

The West holds so much romance and intrigue all wrapped up into one, and today, it still lives in the Town of Cave Creek. Look back thousands of years, the land on which Cave Creek has risen, was home to Native Americans working every bit as hard to preserve their history as the current day resident is doing to preserve the essence of the western existence today.

If you hike in the hills surrounding the town you will still find evidence of the Native Americans, with shards of pottery and arrowheads dotting the land that you both have trekked.

The miners and cattlemen were next and they had it right—seek out the gold, silver and copper and have the perfect location to graze the herd, all at the base of some of the most majestic mountain ranges in the Southwest.

Cave Creek gained its fame during the early 1800's from the men that sought to strike it rich in gold, and the Cavalry soldiers protecting the area from the Apaches who were fighting to save their land, too.

The State of Arizona was formed in 1912, and it took until 1986 before the town of Cave Creek would became incorporated and established as a place where visitors were always welcome.

Bryan's Black Mountain Barbecue joins in the town's history getting part of its name from the incredible mountain just in front of the restaurant. Black Mountain looms high above the town sitting at 3398 feet above the desert floor.

So head on up to the town of Cave Creek, sit at Bryan's Saguaro bar on the patio and you will feel what the town folk felt more than 100 years ago. Enjoy a feast for the eyes, the soul and fulfill your hunger for great Barbecue.

I hope you have enjoyed the tour and now I hope you will try out some of my favorite recipes with your friends and family. The whole idea of the book is to give people a flavor of what we do at Bryan's Black Mountain Barbecue. For me, personally, it's a way to express artistically what we do. I am a chef, yes, but I have a lot of things I want to express about being a chef.

I feel the book is a way to bring everything together and give you a well-rounded idea of what we do here. The main focus is an expression of Bryan's Black Mountain Barbecue in another way—we do more than just cook food and eat food—there are a whole lot of feelings, friendships and textures that go into every bite.

No matter how you get here, Bryan's is worth the ride.

When you find a restaurant you like, it's an experience, there's more to it than eating - it's the feeling you get sitting there, the environment, the distinctive character, the smells, the feeling of people gathering around you, the sites, the sounds—it's the recipe for a good restaurant.

That's a huge factor in how we designed everything. Donna and I talked about all the things we liked about restaurants, we made lists, and we tried to recreate the feeling that we wanted you to experience. There are certain places that give you that comfortable feeling and Bryan's Black Mountain Barbecue is on that list. People don't roam far anymore looking for just the right spot, they have found it in Cave Creek at Bryan's Black Mountain Barbecue. Legends were born in the old west...

Bryan's Black Mountain Barbecue is one for the history books.

INDEX

A
Adria Pentkowski, 102, 103
Artichoke, Fried, Po'Boy with Smoked Tomato Remoulade,
   76, 77
Apples, Root Beer Battered, 90, 91

B
Baked Potato Salad, 82, 83
BBQ SAUCES
   Bryan's BBQ Sauce, 96
   Ginger Beer BBQ Sauce, 69
   Prickly Pear Lime BBQ Sauce, 49
Beans, Six-Pack Cowboy, 80
Beer and Pickled Jalapeño Hushpuppies, 24, 25
BEEF
   Beef Brisket, 61
   Brisket and Black-Eyed Pea Chili, 28
   Brisket Burnt End Grilled Cheese Sandwich, 62, 63
   Brisket Sandwich, 61
BISON
   Pepita Bison Burger topped with Fire Roasted
      Poblano and Shitake Mushrooms, 64
   Sage and Juniper Rubbed Bison Ribs with a Sweet
      Persimmon Glaze, 66, 67
Bryan's Barbecue Chicken, 58, 59
BRYAN'S BBQ PANTRY, 98
Bryan's Barbecue Sauce, 96
Bryan's Big One, 52, 53
Bryan's Cardamom Snickerdoodle
   Ice Cream Sandwich, 88
Bryan's Spice Rub, 97

C
Cardamom Honey, 93
Cave Creek, Arizona, 106-107
CHICKEN
   Bryan's Barbecue Chicken, 58, 59
   Firebird Chicken, 56
   Firebird Chicken Wings, 22, 23
   Pulled Chicken Sandwich, 58
   Spring Chicken Salad Sandwich, 60
CHILI AND STEWS
   Brisket and Black-Eyed Pea Chili, 28
   Cabrito and Chicken Brunswick Stew, 31
   Shrimp Evelyn, 33
Chow Chow, 51
Collard Greens, Rob's 85
Cole Slaw , Rob's Olive, 87

D
DESSERTS
   Root Beer Battered Apples, 90, 91
   Bryan's Cardamom Snickerdoodle Ice Cream
      Sandwich, 88
   Watermelon Wedges with Cardamom Honey, 92, 93

F
Farmers Salad, 86
Firebird Chicken, 56
Firebird Chicken Wings, 22, 23
Firebird Glaze, 22, 56

G
Ginger Beer BBQ Sauce, 69
GLAZES
   Sweet Persimmon Glaze, 66
   Firebird Glaze, 22
Goat (Cabrito), 30

J
Jalapeños, Sweet Pickled, 78

L
Lamb Drumstick with Ginger Beer BBQ Sauce, 68, 69
Las Tiendas, 36, 104, 105
Lemon Pepper Vinaigrette, 27

M
Molasses Dijon Spread, 60, 74

O
Olive Cole Slaw, 87

P
Pantry List, 98
Paul Boruff, 42, 43
Pepita Bison Burger topped with Fire Roasted
   Poblano and Shiitake Mushrooms, 64
Pickled Watermelon Rind, 51
POETRY
   "Barley, Hops, Water and Yeast", 81
   "Genesis Rarebit", 63
   "Get That Barbecue Down", 110
PORK
   Bryan's Big One, 52, 53
   Creeker Ribs with Prickly Pear Lime BBQ Sauce, 49
   Pork Butt, 54
   Pulled Pork Sandwich, 55
   Smoked Sausage Sandwich with Pickled Watermelon
      Rind Chow Chow, 50, 51
   St. Louis Cut Spare Ribs, 46
   The Big Pig, 20, 21
Pork Butt, 54
Pork Sandwich, 55
Potato, Baked Salad, 82, 83
PREPARATION
   Chicken, 50
   Pork Butt, 50
   Brisket, 50

Baby your Brisket, 60
A Good Rub, 97
Prickly Pear Lime BBQ Sauce, 49

R
Ribs, Creeker Ribs with Prickly Pear Lime BBQ Sauce, 49
Ribs, Sage and Juniper Rubbed Bison Ribs with Sweet
Persimmon Glaze, 66, 67
Ribs, St. Louis Cut Spare 46
Ribs of Romaine with Lemon Pepper Vinaigrette, 26, 27
Rob Olson, 102, 103
RUBS
Sage and Juniper Rub, 66
Smoked Salt, 96
Bryan's Spice Rub, 97

S
Salt, Smoked, 96
SAUCES
Bryan's Barbecue Sauce, 96
Ginger Beer BBQ Sauce, 69
Lemon Pepper Vinaigrette, 27
Prickly Pear Lime BBQ Sauce, 49
Smoked Tomato Remoulade, 75
Sausage, Smoked Sausage Sandwich with Pickled
Watermelon Rind Chow Chow, 50, 51
SEAFOOD
Crawfish Mac and Cheese, 83
Shrimp Evelyn, 33
SIDES
Baked Potato Salad, 82, 83
Crawfish Mac & Cheese, 83
Farmers Salad, 86
Olive Cole Slaw for a Crowd, 87
Rob's Collard Greens, 85
Six Pack Cowboy Beans, 80, 81
Sweet Pickled Jalapeños, 78
Shrimp Evelyn, 33
Smoked Tomato Remoulade, 75
SMOKER TIPS
Proper Temperatures, 45
Brisket, 61
Pork, 48
Chicken, 48
Ribs, 48
Rubs, 97
Wood, 99
Squash, Pulled Sandwich, 72
Sweet Pickled Jalapeños, 78
STARTERS
Beer and Pickled Jalapeño Hushpuppies, 24, 25
Firebird Chicken Wings, 22, 23
Firebird Glaze, 22, 56

Ribs of Romaine Salad with Lemon Pepper Vinaigrette
26, 27
The Big Pig, 20, 21
STEW
Shrimp Evelyn, 33
Cabrito and Chicken Brunswick Stew, 31
Summer Tomato Sandwich with Molasses Dijon Spread, ..
73, 74

T
The Big Pig, 20, 21
TOPPINGS
Cardamom Honey, 93
Chow Chow, 51
Fire Roasted Poblano and Shiitake Mushrooms, 64
Lemon Pepper Vinaigrette, 27
Molasses Dijon Spread, 60
Pickled Watermelon Rind, 51

V
VEGGIE
Fried Artichoke Po'Boy with Smoked Tomato
Remoulade, 76, 77
Pulled Squash Sandwich, 72
Summer Tomato Sandwich with Molasses Dijon Spread,
74, 75

W
Watermelon Wedges with Cardamom Honey, 92, 93

Early morning
get the fire on

Red hot coals
down in the ground

Chop the Hickory
and Apple wood

Rub that shoulder
up real good

Barbecue, oh Barbecue
gotta put the Barbecue down

See that meat on
nice and low

In the warm white
hard wood smoke

Not too hot
and not too cold

Watch that meat
down in the hole

Barbecue, oh Barbecue
gotta put the Barbecue down

Vinegar Sauce
that's nice and thin

On the Pork
and soaks right in

Homemade Slaw and
Brown sugar beans

Black-eyed Peas
and Turnip Greens

Barbecue, oh Barbecue
gotta put the Barbecue on

Barbecue, oh Barbecue
gotta put the Barbecue down

GET THAT BARBECUE DOWN

Written by Bryan Dooley, 2008

Bryan Dooley is no stranger to the art of good barbecue. Chef Dooley's love of barbecue encircles every recipe just like the pecan wood smoke that billows around every morsel at Bryan's Black Mountain Barbecue in Cave Creek, Arizona. Dooley brings his restaurant favorites and a look into his childhood and his career through photos, poems, stories and his best recipes that will delight the reader. Chef Dooley gained his knowledge and training from the Culinary Institute of America in Hyde Park, NY. After 13 years with the Fairmont Resort in Scottsdale, it was time to set out on his own developing a barbecue restaurant with countless awards of recognition for the best barbecue in Arizona. Awards include: Best of the Valley, Phoenix Magazine; Best of Phoenix, New Times and Top 10 All American Eats, Arizona Republic, just to name a few. Dooley and his family enjoy all the West has to offer including hiking, rock hounding and of course, the barbecue gatherings with family and friends. Chef Dooley received his undergraduate degree from Northern Arizona University.

Leslie V. Bay is a noted public relations and marketing specialist and award winning writer. She is the recent winner of the 17th Annual Communicator Award 2011 - Silver, judged and overseen by the International Academy of the Visual Arts (IAVA). The Communicator Awards is the leading international awards program honoring creative excellence for communication professionals. In addition, she is a Davey Award Winner for Small Agencies, Big Ideas and winner of The Silver Microphone Award. Bay is a graduate of Arizona State University and is the owner of Bay & Associates, a boutique Public Relations and Marketing agency in Scottsdale, Arizona.

Lori Cowherd brings her accomplished fine arts background to the team. Cowherd is a graduate of California State University, Long Beach, and holds a Master of Arts in Painting and Drawing. She utilized her talents at a top Long Beach design firm for a decade as Senior Art Director on accounts such as Adidas, Nissan and Mercedes Benz. In 2004 she relocated to Arizona and opened The Orange Gourd Design Studio, a freelance web, graphic design and illustration studio. In addition, Cowherd continues her fine arts work, most recently, showing a satirical series in oils, along with thoughtful written commentary, highlighting scandalous figures in politics and high finance.

David Moore has a strong foundation in formal fundamentals of photography inspired by watching Ansel Adams print in his Carmel darkroom. Moore's work can be seen in numerous catalogues and publications, including Bon Appetit, Phoenix Magazine and Phoenix Home and Garden. Moore's love of photography has brought him to teach Fine Art Photography in Los Angeles at various Colleges and Junior Colleges. He produced a workshop for UCLA Extension, "Images without Darkrooms". Now residing in Arizona, he pursues his Commercial Photography interests, which include photography for The Royal Palms Resort Cookbook.

ACKNOWLEDGEMENTS
Thanks to Leslie, Lori and David for all the hard work!
Thanks to Rob and Adria for making it happen!
Thanks to "The Good Guys" Howard and Dave for giving us our look, Steve and Bryan for lighting us up!
Thanks to Jon and Michael for helping us build our dream restaurant!
Thanks to chef Reed for showing me how!
Thanks to all our loyal customers, we wouldn't be here without you!